What Are Patterns in Space?

HOUGHTON MIFFLIN HARCOURT

PHOTOGRAPHY CREDITS: COVER (bg) ©Christophe Lehenaff/Photononstop/Corbis; 3 (c) ©Spirit of America/Shutterstock; (b) ©VanHart/Shutterstock; 4 (b) ©Photodisc/Getty Images; 5 (r) ©Anton Balazh/Shutterstock; 6 (l) ©Albrecht Weiber/imagebroker RF/age fotostock; (r) ©P. Broze & A. Chederros/ONOKY - Photononstop/Alamy Images; 6 (tc) ©sebikus/Shutterstock; 7 (t) ©Joseph Sohm-Visions of America/Stockbyte/Getty Images; 9 (r) ©Stuart Fox/Getty Images; (l) ©gorillaimages/Shutterstock; 10 (b) ©PhotoDisc/Getty Images; 11 (l, r) ©Clifford Rhodes/Alamy Images; 14 (t) ©M. Delpho/Arco Images GmbH/Alamy Images; 16 (b) ©Tristan3D/Shutterstock; 17 (t) ©IMAGINA Photography/Alamy Images; 18 (t) ©Christophe Lehenaff/Photononstop/Corbis; 20 (t) ©Orla/Shutterstock; 21 (b) ©Digital Vision/Getty Images; 22 (t) ©Digital Vision/Getty Images

If you have received these materials as examination copies free of charge, Houghton Mifflin Harcourt Publishing Company retains title to the materials and they may not be resold. Resale of examination copies is strictly prohibited.

Possession of this publication in print format does not entitle users to convert this publication, or any portion of it, into electronic format.

Copyright © by Houghton Mifflin Harcourt Publishing Company

All rights reserved. No part of this work may be reproduced or transmitted in any form or by any means, electronic or mechanical, including photocopying or recording, or by any information storage and retrieval system, without the prior written permission of the copyright owner unless such copying is expressly permitted by federal copyright law. Requests for permission to make copies of any part of the work should be addressed to Houghton Mifflin Harcourt Publishing Company, Attn: Contracts, Copyrights, and Licensing, 9400 Southpark Center Loop, Orlando, Florida 32819-8647.

Printed in U.S.A.

ISBN: 978-0-544-07309-8

3 4 5 6 7 8 9 10 1083 21 20 19 18 17 16 15 14

4500470073   A B C D E F G

Be an Active Reader!

Look for each word in yellow along with its meaning.

rotates	orbit	moon phases
axis	tide	constellation

Underlined sentences answer the questions.
What causes day and night?
How does Earth move?
What are shadows, and how do they change?
What causes the seasons?
What is the moon?
How do the sun, Earth, and the moon work together?
Why does the shape of the moon seem to change?
What are the moon's phases?
Why do the constellations seem to move?
What do we know about other planets?
What else is found in space?

What causes day and night?

In most places, it is light outside in the morning. It stays that way throughout the day. Every night, it gets dark and stays that way until morning. This pattern repeats every day. Why does this pattern happen?

Earth rotates, or turns. It makes one full turn every 24 hours. One part of Earth faces the sun. It's day in that part. The other part faces away from the sun. It's night in that part.

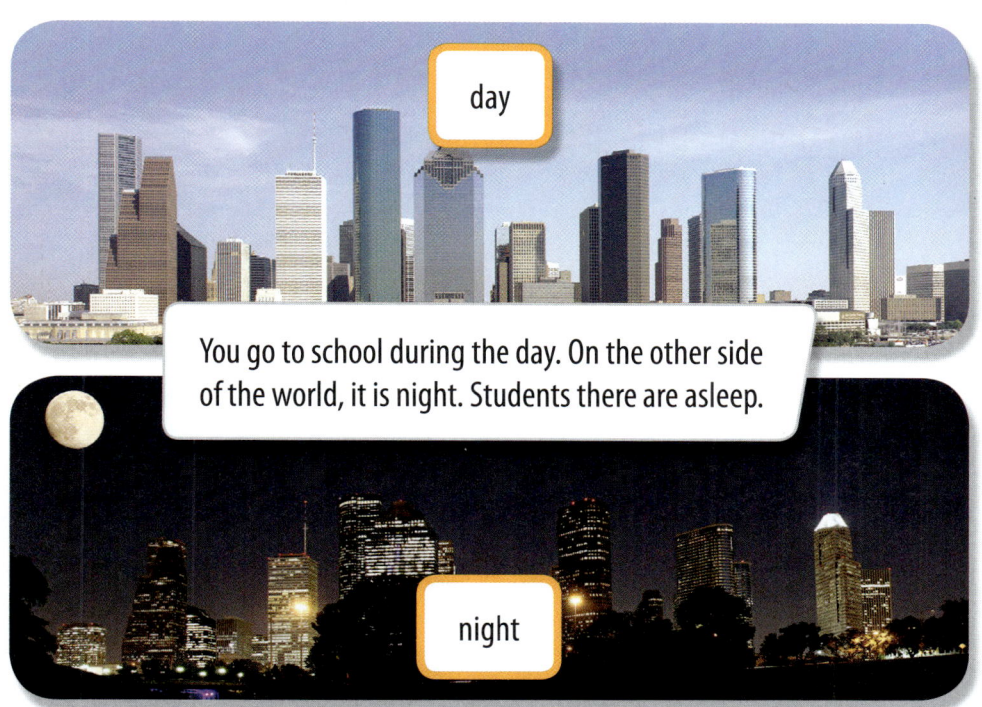

day

You go to school during the day. On the other side of the world, it is night. Students there are asleep.

night

3

How does Earth move?

Earth rotates on its axis. An axis is an imaginary line that goes through Earth from the North Pole to the South Pole.

Think about sticking your finger into the hole of an olive. Your finger is the axis, and the olive is Earth. Now bend your wrist until the axis (your finger) is leaning to the left. Earth tilts on its axis just as your finger is tilting.

Earth makes a complete turn every 24 hours. As it turns, Earth also revolves, or goes around the sun. Every 365 days, Earth completes one orbit around the sun. An orbit is the path of one object in space around another object.

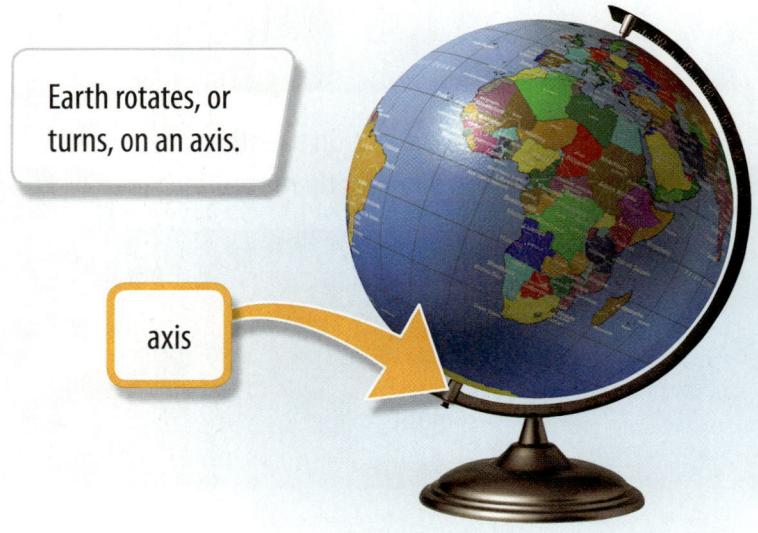

Earth rotates, or turns, on an axis.

axis

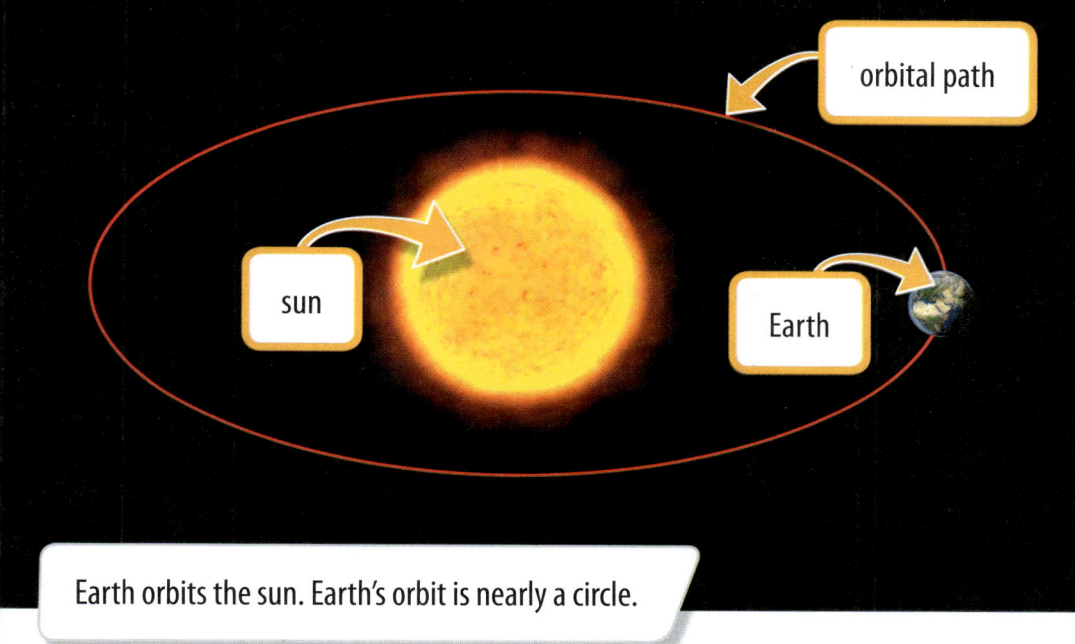

Earth orbits the sun. Earth's orbit is nearly a circle.

The distance between Earth and the sun is about 150 million kilometers (km), or 93 million miles (mi). The orbit that Earth makes is not a perfectly round circle. It's more like a slightly stretched-out circle. The sun sits just off the center of the circle.

The distance between Earth and the sun changes during the year. That's because of the shape of Earth's orbit. Earth and the sun are about 147 million km (91 million mi) apart at their closest point. They are about 152 million km (95 million mi) apart at their farthest point.

What are shadows, and how do they change?

A shadow is a dark area or shape. It's made when an object is between the sun's rays and the ground.

Go outside in the morning and stand in a sunny place. Look down at your shadow. Go back outside at noon to that same spot. Look at your shadow again. What do you see? Look at your shadow again in the late afternoon. What does your shadow look like this time?

Shadows change as the day goes by. They are long in the morning and afternoon. That's because the sun is low in the sky. The sun is right over our heads at noon. Shadows are the shortest at that time of day.

Compare the lengths of the shadows in the photos below. Which photo was taken closer to noon, or the middle of the day? What makes you think so?

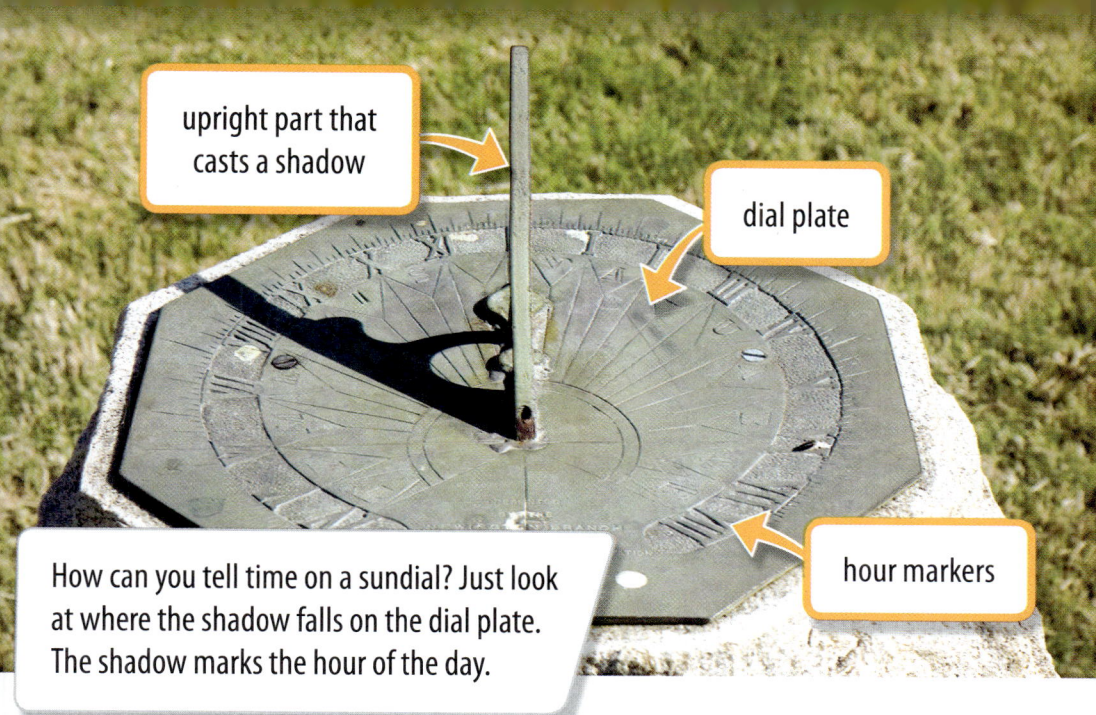

- upright part that casts a shadow
- dial plate
- hour markers

How can you tell time on a sundial? Just look at where the shadow falls on the dial plate. The shadow marks the hour of the day.

Sundials use shadows to show the time of day. The Egyptians created the first sundials thousands of years ago.

A sundial has a bottom piece called a dial plate. The plate is made of metal, wood, or stone. Small lines on the dial plate show the hours of the day. A sundial also has a sticklike part that stands up from the plate. This upright part makes a shadow on the plate. The shadow moves around the dial as Earth rotates. The shadow falls on a new line every hour.

Earth is divided into two halves. The top half is the Northern Hemisphere. The bottom half is the Southern Hemisphere.

What causes the seasons?

The four seasons are spring, summer, fall, and winter. We have seasons because of Earth's tilt and its orbit around the sun.

Imagine a line that divides Earth into two halves. That line is the equator. The half above the line is the Northern Hemisphere. The half below the line is the Southern Hemisphere.

Earth is tilted on its axis. The Northern Hemisphere is tilted toward the sun for about half of the year. During this time, the Northern Hemisphere gets more direct sunlight than the Southern Hemisphere does.

When the Northern Hemisphere is tilted toward the sun, it's summer in that part of the world. It's warm outside. The Southern Hemisphere is tilted away from the sun at this time.

When it's summer where you live, it's winter for people who live below the equator. <u>The seasons are caused by the changes in how sunlight hits the different parts of Earth.</u>

winter

summer

When it's winter for people in the Northern Hemisphere, it's summer for people in the Southern Hemisphere.

9

What is the moon?

The moon is Earth's satellite. A satellite is an object in space that moves around another, larger object. The moon does not have air, wind, or liquid water. Its surface is covered in craters. Craters are pits, or dents in the surface of the moon. The craters are made when objects in space crash into the moon.

The moon looks large to us because it is close. It is only one-fourth the size of Earth. The moon is the second-brightest object in the sky, after the sun. The moon does not make its own light, however. It simply reflects the sun's light.

Craters cover the surface of the moon. There are also mountains and large areas called "seas." These are really just flat areas, or plains.

Earth has a force called gravity. Gravity pulls things toward Earth's center. Earth's gravity keeps us from floating above the ground. The moon has gravity, too.

The moon's gravity pulls on Earth. This force affects Earth's ocean as the moon revolves around Earth. The moon's gravity makes the level of the water rise and fall. The rising and falling of the water is called the **tide**. Each day, there is a high tide. Each day, there is a low tide.

High tide happens when the water level is the highest. Low tide happens when the water level is the lowest.

high tide

low tide

11

Throw a ball up in the air. What happens next? Gravity makes the ball come down.

How do the sun, Earth, and the moon work together?

Earth rotates on its axis every 24 hours, which is one day. Earth orbits the sun, which takes one year. The moon rotates on its own axis, too. One rotation on the moon's axis takes about a month. The moon also orbits Earth in the same amount of time. Because of the moon's and Earth's rotations and orbits, we always see the same side of the moon.

What keeps the sun, Earth, and the moon from colliding into one another or floating off into space? Gravity! Gravity is the force that keeps the sun, Earth, and the moon in place.

The sun, Earth, and the moon work together as a system. A system is a set of things that work together as parts of a whole. Without each part, the system would not work. What would happen if the sun were no longer part of the system? People, plants, and animals depend on the sun for light and warmth. What if the orbit of the moon changed? How might a change in the tides affect animals and plants that live in the oceans?

Facts About the Sun, Earth, and Moon System		
	Size	Motion
Sun	1,391,000 km (864,400 mi) in diameter	• Center of revolution of other objects in the solar system
Earth	12,756 km (7,926 mi) in diameter	• Rotates once every 24 hrs • Orbits sun once about every 365 days
Moon	3,475 km (2,159 mi) in diameter	• Rotates once about every 27 days • Orbits Earth once about every 27 days

The light of the moon is a reflection of the sun's light.

Why does the shape of the moon seem to change?

When you look at the moon on different nights, it looks like its shape has changed. The shape doesn't really change. The moon reflects the light from the sun. As the moon revolves around Earth, half of the moon is always lighted. What we see depends on where the moon and Earth are in their orbits around the sun. The changes we see are called moon phases.

You can try an activity that shows what causes the moon to have phases. You will need a globe, a ball, a small lamp or flashlight, and two friends. Work in a darkened room.

Find North America on the globe. Ask one friend to turn on the lamp or flashlight. Face North America to the light. Ask your other friend to hold the ball between the globe and the lamp or flashlight. How much of the lighted side of the ball do you see?

Keep the lamp or flashlight where it is. Ask your friend to move the ball around the globe a few inches. How much of the lighted side of the ball do you see now?

Ask your friend to keep moving the ball around the globe. Note how the lighted part of the ball changes. This is like the "changing shape" of the moon!

These students are modeling different phases of the moon.

Earth

moon

sun

15

What are the moon's phases?

There are eight phases of the moon. Four are main phases.

New moon. The moon is between the sun and Earth. All three objects are lined up. The lighted side of the moon is facing away from us. We can't see it.

Full moon. Earth is between the moon and the sun. We see all of the lighted side of the moon. It looks like a full circle.

First quarter and third quarter. The moon is at a 90-degree angle to the sun and Earth. We see half of the lighted side. This is also known as a half-moon. It looks like a half-circle.

There are eight phases of the moon.

Do you know what a "blue moon" is? It is the second of two full moons in one month. We do not often see a blue moon.

There are phases between the four main phases of the moon. One of these in-between phases is called the crescent moon. A crescent moon looks like a banana. It is smaller than a quarter moon. We see less than a half-moon.

Another in-between phase is the gibbous moon. This shape of the moon is bigger than a half-moon, but less than a full moon.

The words *waxing* and *waning* tell whether the lighted part of the moon is getting bigger or smaller. For example, the waxing gibbous phase comes between the first quarter and the full moon. The waning gibbous phase comes between the full moon and the third quarter.

The Little Dipper is part of the constellation *Ursa Minor*. The Big Dipper is part of the constellation *Ursa Major*.

Little Dipper

Big Dipper

Why do the constellations seem to move?

A constellation is a group of stars. Cygnus the Swan, Taurus the Bull, and Leo the Lion are constellations in the night sky. There are 88 constellations.

People long ago looked at the stars and saw pictures. They gave the constellations names. Different cultures gave the constellations different names. Today, we use the names the Greek and Roman peoples used.

Constellations seem to move in the sky. You don't see the same constellations in the summer that you do in the winter. Remember that Earth is always moving. This means that you'll see different constellations in different seasons. It all depends on where Earth is in its orbit around the sun.

Think about how the equator divides Earth into two halves. Some constellations can be seen only from above the equator. Some can be seen only from below the equator. Some can be seen from both halves of Earth. For example, people above and below the equator can see the constellation named Orion.

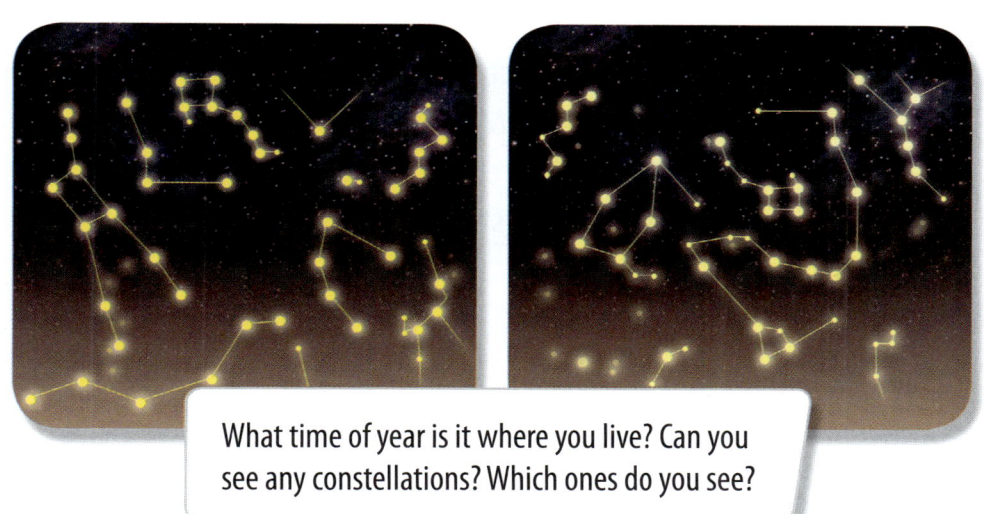

What time of year is it where you live? Can you see any constellations? Which ones do you see?

19

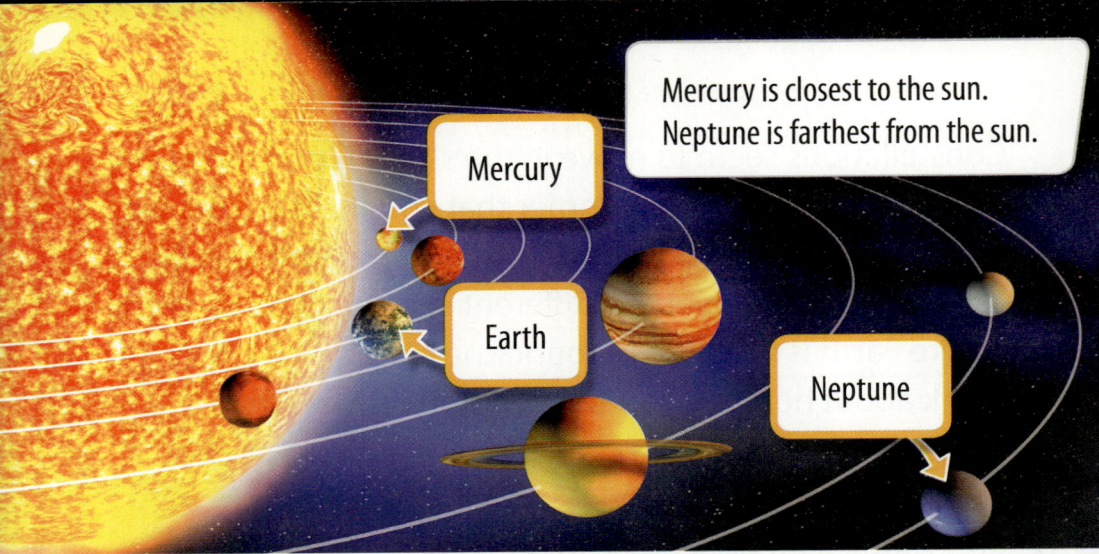

What do we know about other planets?

Mercury, Venus, Earth, Mars, Jupiter, Saturn, Uranus, and Neptune are all planets. They all orbit the sun. Most have at least one moon.

Pluto used to be called a planet. Its orbit is different from the orbits of the others. It's smaller, too. Scientists have decided that Pluto should be called a dwarf planet.

Mercury, Venus, Earth, and Mars are solid and rocky. They are closer to the sun than the rest. Jupiter, Saturn, Uranus, and Neptune are made up mostly of gases. They each have many moons.

Earth takes one year to complete an orbit of the sun. The other planets take different amounts of time. This means that a day on Earth is not the same length as a day on Venus.

Scientists have observed that Venus has plains and mountains. These scientists think that the plains and mountains were made by lava from volcanoes. Some of Earth's plains and mountains were made by volcanoes, too. Earth is cooler than Venus, though. The temperature on Venus's surface is almost 482 °Celsius (900 °Fahrenheit)! That's hot enough to melt many metals.

Venus is almost the same size as Earth. It is rocky and solid like Earth.

21

We last saw Halley's comet in 1986. We won't see it again until 2061.

What else is found in space?

The sun, moon, and planets are found in space. Comets, asteroids, and meteors are in space, too.

A comet is made of rock and frozen gases. Comets orbit the sun. The most famous comet is Halley's comet. Halley's comet takes about 76 years to go around the sun.

Asteroids are chunks of rock and metal. They also go around the sun. There are lots of asteroids in space. They are found mostly between Mars and Jupiter.

Pieces of asteroids sometimes break off. They move through space. Sometimes the pieces come into Earth's atmosphere. They start to burn. Then they're called meteors. When many meteors fall into Earth's atmosphere at once, we have a meteor shower.

Responding

Make an Argument

For many years, Pluto was on the list of planets. In 2006, it was taken off the list. Now Pluto is called a dwarf planet. Which type of planet do you think Pluto should be? Work with a partner to find out more information about Pluto. Use the Internet or the library. Decide if you think Pluto should be listed as a planet or a dwarf planet. Then pick another pair of researchers and debate your opinions. Use reasons and information from your research to support your opinion.

Write a Brochure

Use the Internet and library to find facts about a scientist who studies space. Write notes about the scientist. Make a list of his or her accomplishments. Then use your notes to design a brochure. It should show a picture of the scientist. Your text should explain who the scientist is and what he or she studies. You should include information on what the scientist has contributed to the study of space. Share your brochure with the class.

Glossary

axis [AK•sis] The imaginary line around which Earth rotates. *We have night and day because Earth turns on its axis.*

constellation [kahn•stuh•LAY•shuhn] A group of stars that seems to form a picture or design in the sky. *Canis Major is a constellation in the shape of a big dog.*

moon phases [MOON FAYZ•iz] Changes in the appearance of the moon's shape as it orbits Earth. *A full moon and a new moon are moon phases.*

orbit [AWR•bit] The path of one object in space around another object. *Each planet follows a different orbit around the sun.*

rotates [ROH•tayts] Turns about an axis. *Venus rotates at a different speed from that of Earth.*

tide [TYD] The rise and fall in the water level of the ocean. *Water covers up part of the beach at high tide.*